YOU
THE BELOVED
THE ONE

YOU
THE BELOVED
THE ONE

Welcome Home

Sue Cawthorne

Copyright © 2022 by Sue Cawthorne

All rights reserved. No part of this book may be reproduced in any form on by an electronic or mechanical means, including information storage and retrieval systems, without permission in writing from the author, except by a reviewer who may quote brief passages in a review. For permission requests, write to the author at "suecawthorne061@gmail.com".

First Edition

Text originally formatted by Laura Renee Stansfield

Book formatted and book cover design by Salah-Eddin Gherbi

ISBN 978-1-3999-3045-1

GRATITUDE

I appreciate your overwhelming beauty, wisdom, love,
all seeing-ness, truth,
and infinite eternal nature.

Thank you for revealing this wonder to me –
for allowing me to see this sweet one that we all are.
I thank every single one of you who has ever lived,
is living and who will live in the future.

Table of Contents

Authentic Self - Real You 8

Natural Awareness 26

One-ness 36

Joy and Ecstasy 46

Awakening Humanity 52

Sleeping Unawakened 64

Truth and Illusion 72

Cosmic Consciousness - Heart Awareness 92

Being Home 104

Love and Intimacy 112

Authentic Self

Real You

Authentic Self - Real You

In each heart there is an inner knowing of wisdom and truth.
Each of us is engaged in a wonderful unfolding
of undreamed of potential.
The authentic you, is the you that is found at your absolute core.
The real you.
The you you were born as.
The amazing you where all the beauty lives.
Where all the love comes from.
The you that knows who you truly are.
The you merging with the forest, the animals and the oceans, the ancestors and the birds.

The great thing is that the real you is fine the way it is.
It can never be destroyed
and it never needs fixing, or mending, or analyzing.
The real you is absolutely intact, and always is.

It is the you that existed before, and will remain, when life's pains, pleasures and dramas have passed away.
It is the you that requires you to be real.
You already have everything you need to live in this world –
as the authentic you.

Authentic Self - Real You

Your authentic self is what you are.
It is always fully accessible to you.

The edges of the you that you have identified yourself as being,
Can consciously extend themselves enormously.
You are seeing and knowing it's nothing to do-ness.
It's totally trusting every living moment,
whether or not it is classed by you into some former category;

Unpleasant, ecstatic, boring, interesting, loving or awful.
Any sort of concept immediately interrupts flow.
It is really about complete rest.
Not even caring about how aware you are.
You are already aware all the time,
and the only problem any of us have is when we deny it.
In this world we have been trained to deny it.
We are consciousness in denial of our clear and perfect awareness.

We have barely recognised what we are.
Now you know that you are already okay
And don't have to try to do or be any different
from how you already are being.

Authentic Self - Real You

Sometimes the feelings of discomfort are so powerful
that you want them to stop.
Sometimes you can experience pleasure and bliss,
which feels like it could last for ever.
Nothing does.
It all comes and goes.
We get to keep nothing.
We already have everything.
Everything changes constantly.
Not wanting to feel so terrible only seems to keep it there.
Holding onto pleasure is also impossible.
No experience lasts and just like sand cannot be held in your hands,
But simply sifts through your fingers.
Simply allowing it to be there allows it to dissolve
Moment to moment
Becoming anything it moves into.
It feels like the edge of nothing and everything.

Allowing one thing –

Authentic Self - Real You

be it a thought, feeling, mood or attitude
to dominate any other is crazy.
The more you scramble your brain trying to achieve a conclusion
or a knowing about anything -
The more you will split your consciousness at your core
and experience separation.

It's like this is it.
Nothing to do.
It may appear that there are two distinct separate awarenesses.
Both okay and yet one and the same consciousness.
The error has been in believing that one is true and the other is not.
There is no erroneous consciousness but only mistaken identity.
Beyond concepts and ever-changing thoughts and feelings
is an extraordinary human consciousness
Which is the innate birthright of everyone.
This is what so many teachers and gurus
and founders of religions and ideologies have perceived,
A consciousness which is interwoven with everyday life,
and every human experience.
We really have the awareness to see ourselves truly
as we already are.

Authentic Self - Real You

Being the real us is easy.
It requires no effort,
But we have been trained and encouraged
to try and struggle from very early on.
And the over-riding belief and fear of many individuals is that
they will never be enough and are inherently imperfect.
Our false identity is hooked up irrevocably with fault,
Imperfection, guilt, pain, suffering and separation.
Lets face it,
If our identity is screwed up from the outset,
then of course we are never going to get there,
Achieve enough, and will always be trying to sort ourselves out –
Which of course will never, ever be enough.
We, as separate split identities of one complete whole,
will never be enough.
However, when an individual person discovers
their own true authentic nature –
the world looks very different to them.

the eternal and infinite all –
We merge with every other living cell in creation.

Authentic Self - Real You

We come from freedom and love.
It is our essence and our true nature.
It's what we are made of.
It's free and it's beautiful and we all are already that.
There is no-one or nothing that is not made
of the same stuff as you and me.
Everything IS this eternal essence.
Here there is no separation at all. Ever.

It's impossible, as we are one interconnected Consciousness.
I am surrounded by Divinity – for want of a better name.
There is nowhere to look.
Everything is right here right now.
Always.
No mystery.

The truth is that you are already okay, already perfect right now.
The lie is that you are anything other than total perfection.
We are now, we always have been and always will be.
Everyone has an awesome awareness
that is ever-present at all times.
It is not dependent on whether you believe in it or not.

Authentic Self - Real You

It just is.
It doesn't depend on how good you think you've been
or how you may think you have failed.
This consciousness is that of life itself.
Every single atom in the Universe shares this awareness
with everything and everyone in it.
This innate consciousness is becoming increasingly recognised
by people of all nations.

It does not belong to any particular religious, philosophical
or spiritual path, belief system or doctrine.
Like the sky it cannot be contained,
And is the true property of everything in existence.
It cannot be controlled and its natural benefit is to give
a greater freedom and expression to any individual
Anywhere, anytime and imbue them with a fresh experience of life,
Whatever the circumstances.
A true experience that we are already perfect,
already okay, right now.

Authentic Self - Real You

We are so used to thinking that we have to instigate change
to move things around,
So that they fit our picture of a preferred state of affairs.
Our innate consciousness is situated
in the frontal lobes of the brain.
It does not need to be developed as it is all seeing and knowing.
It has an intelligence which is not limited by linear time and space
Eternity and infinity are 'the norm' here.
Past and future belong to a fractured consciousness
in which we will never feel okay.
I thank you and I acknowledge you.
You are already 100% perfect right now just the way you are –
Whoever, whatever and wherever you are.
It has no bearing on what you may think about yourself.

True identity unfolding into real perception
and authentic expression of the individual person.
But yet again individual and separate are poles apart
in definition and meaning.
Time is non-existent and the past and future don't come into it.

Authentic Self - Real You

You were born with it.
Your little baby face beamed out your true consciousness
to everyone and everything.
When others saw you they found your radiance
and openness awesome.
You were still so connected to your true awareness,
it was all you knew.
And in this world of blindness,
You awakened and reminded people,
of who you are and who they are.
You reflected a true reflection back into a world,
where distortion abounds.

You knew you were the Beloved, the One.
And you knew that everyone and everything was the Beloved too.
You experienced yourself as the sea of Bliss
that is spoken of in all spiritual writings and teachings.
Now you can return to that bliss bathed state of awareness
and continue to grow in it
And allow it to blossom and flower in you now as an adult.
That baby awareness can now grow up and mature
And transform your whole existence.

Authentic Self - Real You

You will be free to now live fully as an adult
for the first time since your babyhood.
Free to experience sheer joy at being alive.
To know the wonder of being in a body – all your bodies.
Free to experience life as it is,
moment by moment,
And not covered and crowded by your personal identity and story.
That was never you and never will be.
This consciousness occurs spontaneously
when all effort of maintaining the false identity are released.

All that is left is the pure aliveness of your true consciousness.
True consciousness then begins to infuse the outer bodies
And life is lived from the inside
and expressed through to the outside.
Now there is a natural flow,
and doing and behaving are expressed from the real you.

True identity being lovingly expressed.
Previously, doing and behaving came from an outer need
to preserve your false identity and supply it
With desires arising from the emotional needs and addictions.

Authentic Self - Real You

The main event is simple.

Being alive is simply your whole being,
honouring what actually is.
Your life is not for your unnatural self
to live a distorted life through.
It's for your glorious real self to live in.

We can embrace what we have always known
was our real consciousness.
It is empty, colourless, nothingness.
Contentless Awareness.
It's the void, the abyss, the cavern of everything that is,
and everything that is not.
Trying to live a meaningful life doesn't work
because it's a life that is lived at the expense of something else.
The only thing that's worth living for.
A huge sacrifice we make.
There's nothing else to do or be now.
We are that already and there was never anything
to get, change, reach or improve.
It's the same for everyone. Already got it.

Authentic Self - Real You

All of us already, with us the only realness to be found.
Did you make your own body? Or did you just find yourself in it?
You just seemed to come into existence as a someone,
who was separate to billions of other someones.
The efforting was the big problem.
The world outside us encourages fake identity
and says you are worthless without one.

The world, hellbent on corrupting
the purity of our natural awareness.
It's an upside down topsy turvy world,
where appearances can readily deceive.

All that glitters is not gold
even in so-called spiritual organizations and teachings.
Many simply wrap a new false identity
on top of the old discarded one.

Consciousness as it is has no separate drive, ambition
or desires to satisfy, as it is totally complete and whole in itself.
It exists in a different medium of being
Than our usual separate 'I' consciousness.

Authentic Self - Real You

And the medium it rests in, is the source of life itself.

It's like looking into a mirror
and merging completely into your own reflection —
Without having the observing part of you
taking any notice of what it sees.
Just ' being ' with things exactly the way they are.
It is the awareness and natural intelligence of love,
for its own sake alone.
This awareness of love has no subject as it is love itself.

You are already more than you could ever dream of.
When realized — you discover that your whole life
has been a senseless struggle against your natural self
and the ease of relaxing into a beautiful existence
no matter what the external world is doing around you.
When you do nothing and stop trying — you are perfect.
It's like a great cosmic joke really.

You have everything — are everything — you thought you wanted
Already.

Authentic Self - Real You

The lie is that there is a 'You' and 'I' at all.
There isn't.
And there is.
It's the clinging to this thought or concept
which continues our fictional incomplete existence.
The mind is terrified of being Nothing.
It thinks it is death.
It's actually the beginning of real life.
Being nothing is the ending of false separation and identity.
The more your consciousness opens up –
the more real becomes your experience of life.
Your sensitivity increases.
Your experience of everything human is experienced more intensely
Because you are really present in life.

What is this picture or image we have of ourselves?
Take a look at what it is based on.
Where does it have its origins?

It comes from outside the real us,
and like an oasis in the desert, lures and entices us

Authentic Self - Real You

into our own personal mirage.

What we see, hear, touch, taste, smell, feel and think
are at the effect of past experiences and conditioning.

A particular part of the brain is responsible for
recording everything in great detail.
Everything is recorded through a filter of a 'me',
and therefore is a personal point of view, of any situation.
Most people view the world through their own personal viewpoint.
Therefore it is a distorted version of events.

It is about comparison, and depending on what identity
the individual has given themselves,
the world will be viewed through that aperture.
In the exact same situation,
two people in the same location at the same time
Will relate entirely different versions of events,
and personal experience.
No two people are the same in history,
experience, conditioning and identity.

Everyone in the world is right now experiencing

Authentic Self - Real You

a different reality to everyone else.

No-one is right and no-one is wrong.
Together we share the human experience.
What I am talking about is the possibility
of You relaxing into your natural self.

Natural Awareness

Natural Awareness

Innate natural awareness, totally perfect and ever-present always.
Whole and complete awareness is what we already are.
We're done, and cannot be improved.
Any philosophy which tells you
there is something to do or change is not true.
It immediately tells you the lie that you are not okay already
And that you have to do something to get better or improve.
Absolutely perfect right now.
Innate awareness just is perfect
and we are the total embodiment of it always.

The very thing we are looking for is present with us all the time.
We are constantly looking for something outside of ourselves,
When it is actually our own true selves we are seeking.
What you are looking for is what you already are.
Experiencing this joyful complete ecstasy –
Is nearer than touching, seeing, breathing, tasting or hearing.

You can truly be with yourself right now in this moment.
To know and merge with your real beauty
is possible anytime, anyplace.
We can have ourselves right now in this moment

Natural Awareness

which blends into all moments forever.
Embrace yourself with true love, appreciation and acceptance.
You are beautiful and perfect the way you are right now
And absolutely ready to love yourself.

At some point it all means nothing and we are thrown back
on our true awareness.
It's beautiful, and our true self will never abandon us.
In fact its our truest and best friend – even if it doesn't feel like it.
It is also our most loving and loyal teacher.
When our position in life is threatened
or when our identity is crushed,
Our true identity will be so close by loving us graciously.

There are in fact two completely different ways of seeing
or perceiving our lives.
This existence and what's happening now.
One way which is lived by the majority of us is about
who we think we are, a false identity
which is based on everything that has happened to us
up to the present time.

Natural Awareness

Our outer experience has coloured
the whole picture of a fictional us.

We, of course, are a machine – everything reacting
and responding to a set of survival mechanisms and patterns
which have secured our existence up to the present time.

We keep them strong and fight
for their continued existence at any cost.
Anyone or anything can be a threat
to the survival of the fictional person
we have had thrust upon us and have worked hard to maintain.
Also everyone has a nice side to their fictional self –
but often there is manipulation and control games going on
behind the convincing smiles.
The 'me' we have come to believe and feel we are.

Our supposed selves.

On a larger scale, that's what wars are.
Defending a fictional split
in the false perception of a fragmented world.

Natural Awareness

There are no splits and the outer world, as well as the inner,
are actually both whole and are the same,
One.

A split second away from your present consciousness
is the plain simple honouring of just being here.
Nothing else to do.

You are naturally clear seeing.
The Holy Grail, Heaven
Samadhi and Nirvana are present always.
There is no search or quest.
You are already these things and more.
That idea is another burden and a tunnel,
with no cheese at the end of it.
The truth is, that you are perfect right now, just the way you are.
Going home starts with complete acceptance of what is –
everything.
From that place the doorway to a true consciousness
can start to open up.
It's as simple as that.

Natural Awareness

Two distinct consciousnesses which operate.
One of them is lying and the other is truth itself.
Which one do you think that most of us let run the show
– which is our lives?
One gives us a false feeling of separateness,
in a transitory existence,
Constant struggle and striving to get somewhere and be somebody.
Distorted reality is what your senses feed back to you.
A place of constant craving from the outside world –
There to serve us with our every need.

We look for outer comfort
In an attempt to connect with our true selves.

Our authentic consciousness gives us permeating peace, trust,
and a whole view of reality –
Life as it really is.
The place we feel completely at home,
Held in the arms of an awesome love and knowing that we too,
Are that love itself.
It's like quenching a thirst that has never been met before.
And it's free and available to us always –

Natural Awareness

No matter what the outside looks like.
No matter what's going on in our lives.
There are in actuality, no excuses
that are a valid reason not to be real.
However meeting your true consciousness begins
The end of your life as you have known it before.
The 'me' you falsely believed yourself to be,
just doesn't have credibility anymore.
As you now know yourself
to be an infinite eternal creator of the Universe.

You are free and without limits or boundaries.

You are fully connecting with the source you came from –
And that source is the softest, tenderest, safest place
you have ever experienced,
Yet you always knew existed.
Your true consciousness is inhabiting
a temporary physical, emotional, mental and etheric body,
for a limited number of years
On this planet.
Earth.

Natural Awareness

The only definite thing you can know for certain,
is that your physical body will die.
When you die, nothing of this world you have lived in,
can be taken with you.
Yet many people struggle, a large percentage of their lives,
to amass so many things, possessions, wealth etc.
Yet it remains behind, after they die.

Everything here is of a temporary nature.
Everything changes constantly.
The outer world is just like a movie,
with chapters and history and stories.
What if it all stopped –
All that outer noise just finished?

Imagine no dramas.

No guilt about the past.
No worries about tomorrow
No expectations.
No longer 'my' or 'your' concern.

Natural Awareness

A lot of people might think that thinking like this
was relinquishing responsibility.
Yet our false sense of duty and responsibility
Are tainted with so much which is added to our compassion.

Far from separating you from everyday life, the true consciousness
you possess allows you a truer experience of reality.
A freshness in the most ordinary everyday events and interactions
with the world

Enriched with newness, awe and childlike wonder.
True connections with your surroundings and relationships,
start to emerge.
It seems to the taster of truth, that previous to their awakening,
They have been in a hypnotic trance,
In a dreamlike state,
All of their lives.

Indeed, like waking up and seeing everything you are,
And all that truly is
For the very first time.
It's overwhelming, with its simplicity and just-is-ness.

Natural Awareness

I can see a time when this is considered normal for everyone.
When people realize effortlessly, that we are not separate,
finite beings, but all One infinite consciousness.

That something deep within you
which you sense is always present and always true and real.
The authentic knowing of pure awareness.
Your natural awareness,
which just knows that all is well whatever may be happening.
This awareness belongs to another part of the brain –
The part which has nothing at all to do with time, memory,
problem solving, analysis, or personal identity.
It's common sense, or just what real intelligence knows.
If we look at the world as a whole we can see easily,
the way that every single part of nature is interconnected.
If suddenly the air disappeared all life would end.
If there was suddenly no water on the planet all life would end.
Everything is interdependent.
If it wasn't for our ancestors we wouldn't be here

One-ness

One-ness

One consciousness shared by all life.
Communion is a constant.
This consciousness shared by us all and by everything in existence
Is the all pervading presence of love itself.
There is just the One of us.
There always was and always will be.
This permanent consciousness is all there really is.

Concepts cannot convey truth.
The mind cannot perceive truth.
It lives in a finite reality of linear time.

Our pervading and totally connected consciousness
is ever-present always.
You and life itself are One.
You are the same and all of creation shares the same soul.
Bring this knowing with you into everyday life.
Into getting up and having breakfast and also knowing
that you and the brightest star in the Heavens
Share the same authentic self.
Welcome Home.

One-ness

Whatever else we hear in our heads –
say yes to embracing and knowing
the tremendously wondrous creation that we are.

The outer Buddha awakens and rouses
the complete enlightened inner Buddha
Which we all already are.
The outer Christ awakens the universal
Love and compassion of our inner Christ.
We are all inclusive beings.
We all died on the cross.
We all received enlightenment under the banyan tree.
We all wrote the Gita, the Vedas and the Bible.
We have all been around every historic event
Experiencing everything and being everybody.

The mistaken belief that there is actually an 'us' –
A separate me – is a big misunderstanding,
At the core of so much confusion, isolation and fear on this planet.
We contain every single experience within us.
All that has gone and all that is to come.

One-ness

You are already more valuable and precious than
Anything the world can give to you.
You are the most wonderful being now.
You are of the greatest worth.
More than anything you could buy, achieve, succeed at
or be powerful and famous for.
You have everything now
That you could spend a lifetime trying to gain yet never find.
You are the greatest gift you can give to yourself.

Now that I experience this reality and know myself not only
as the human being I live as,
But the whole of life too.
Being, source, truth, reality.
What we truly all are.
There is nowhere to look and no mountain to climb.
Everything is right here right now.
No mystery and no journey.
The journey is just another mirage containing no fresh source
of water to refresh your thirst.

One-ness

I am willing to embrace and experience our magnificent energy and
completely enjoy it along with all of life.
There's just the one of us.
It only appears in the physical world that there are billions of us.
In dimensions invisible to most of us
there is union and oneness.
We are waking up to this truth more and more.
Truth does not know separation and neither does love.
Love is the ultimate truth.

Real love which is complete in itself and requires, nor has need of,
anything or anyone.
I know and see manifest in this world the beauty and perfection
that is our true consciousness,
Our clear perception,
without the veils of conditioning and confusion.

You merge into everything – but you are not identified with yourself
in the way you are familiar with.
Your individuality as you have previously experienced it
is nowhere to be found.
Now you experience yourself without boundaries and separation.

One-ness

You recognise your wholeness.
Your past personal history is no longer running the show.
The agendas are gone along with all the games and control
Which keep alive the separating strategies in this world of one-ness.

This is true relaxation.
You completely let yourself be held in the love
and safety that you are.
I am the Beloved,
I am my own lover.
You are the Beloved,
You are your own lover.
We are the Beloved,
You are the one that you have been searching for all your life.

Remain with the deepest of all connections
And know the most tender, beautiful and intimate connection
You can ever make with your own true self.

Emptiness is filled with complete love.
I am the Beloved.
You are the Beloved.

One-ness

We are the Same.

Our energy and life force have been misdirected for millennia.

We have evolved accessing only a small part
of our intelligence and consciousness.
As a species we have specialized particular skills and talents.
Often people who are open to levels of awareness and intelligence
outside the range of what is considered normal
are ostracized, ridiculed, feared or revered.
We exercise the herd behaviour.
With all the leaps in technology today, is there really true evolution
of the species in any way measurable
In terms of compassion and true humanity?
We all need a break.
Everyone.
Its just too much for everyone the way things are.
Even if you are very rich and successful,
You already know that your life's efforting,
Has taken you nowhere.
All that trying, and still no happier – or even less happy –
than you were.
Our true intelligence is whole and complete already.

One-ness

As a species we have the opportunity to connect with it
Now, in our lifetime.
We all have the opportunity to be part
of an evolutionary re-birth of human consciousness.

Just being.
You are being true consciousness.
This is not some rare state for the special few anymore.
In fact being restful in your own skin and being present
is just a very healthy state to be in.
Any other state is one of distortion and opinion.
It's not whole and complete.

It's as though our naturally healthy birthright
of a loving peaceful existence has got lost somewhere.
All the time it hasn't gone anywhere.
Just like the Sun behind a cloud.
Our consciousness,
The consciousness we all share which is only One.

One-ness

Here you are at the main event of your life.
All the rest of your life has been the sideshows.
Until now you had been unaware that there was a main event.
The main event is simple.
Easier than anything else you have ever done.
That's because it requires no effort
other than to relax, relax and relax right into yourself.
You don't have to change anything
at all.
Any effort will make it impossible.

At the core of you, deep inside, you are able to reconnect
with the real truth of yourself.
At your core you are connected to the source of yourself.
They are the same.
We are all expressions of one consciousness.

Joy and Ecstasy

Joy and Ecstasy

Ecstasy has become a forgotten language.
Ecstasy is the language of our authentic real self.
Ecstasy is described as 'a state of overwhelming delight, rapture,
an intense state of any emotion.'
Ecstasy derives from the Greek 'existanai'
which means 'to displace' or drive out of one's senses.
That is the key to ecstasy.

It drives one out of their sense of ego or thought centred experience
- Into a place where they can enter the mystery directly.
The experience of ecstasy allows us to make a distinction
between the authentic self
As opposed to the conceptual self -
A self which is socially constructed.

The Truth has been hidden
It begins with the individual.
You, your family, your friends.
You are all already fine and totally okay.
You don't need fixing.
You have access to an amazing awareness.
The same awareness as Jesus, Buddha

Joy and Ecstasy

and leaders of world faiths and religions
An awareness that has been viewed as special.
It's not.
It's already present.
It's our innate consciousness.
It's our complete whole intelligence.
An awareness that has been elevated to sainthood, guruhood.
Everyone is already that.

We are told we are imperfect.
That's a lie from the very beginning of our existence.
We are controlled and programmed into thinking
that we are not pure, beautiful embodiments of Life itself.
We have become slaves.
We are living in a prison.
The world has become our cage.
We don't even have to escape though.
We are free already.
Let's celebrate such awesome truth – Wow!

People take drugs to get in touch with what's already inside them.
Where do those experiences come from?

Joy and Ecstasy

From what you are already.
It's not necessary to change anything or improve.
You are okay now.
Resurrection.
Of the world,
Of our natures,
Of our reality,
Of our true identity.
One consciousness,
One life –
True Intelligence.

To live one day of miracles is more beautiful
and worthwhile than to live 1,000 years denying that wonder.
I receive and say yes, yes, yes.
It is the voice of all of us deep within.

We live in a miraculous world.
All hearts beat as one.
The Universe we inhabit sees itself
and in its seeing loves itself completely.
Enraptured in itself.

Joy and Ecstasy

Miracles are happening every moment.
They happen eternally, naturally.
The whole of this life is one huge miracle

The real you knows that you are
the Creator of the entire Universe.
You know eternity and infinity and that time is non existent.
Your natural state is to rest in your true nature and enjoy it.
Our true nature IS Joy.
Our true nature is celebratory of all life.
Here we experience being all of existence
without having any opinion about any of it.

Awakening Humanity

Awakening Humanity

Now that I experience this reality and know myself not only
as the human being I live as,
But the whole of life too.
Being, source, truth, reality.
What we truly all are.
There is nowhere to look and no mountain to climb.
Everything is right here right now.
No mystery and no journey.
The journey is just another mirage containing no fresh source
of water to refresh your thirst.

I look forwards to the day when all of humanity celebrates all of life.
The day when we awaken as a planet
and natural consciousness is expressed
As the one we are.
In a state of natural enthrallment and wonder.
When the simplest pebble and the most perfect diamond
are viewed as equal
Because we are aware that they are made of the same stuff.
Perfection.
Nothing else exists but this.
Awesome appreciation and overflowing

Awakening Humanity

Wonder and gratitude for this life,
This existence.

We all have the capacity to know ourselves, to appreciate ourselves,

To fall madly in love with ourselves.

Can you imagine being head over heels in love with yourself?
So in love in fact that you see nothing but perfection in yourself
And everyone and everything –
Regardless of whatever you might be thinking or feeling.
Taking this a step forwards, can you imagine adoring yourself?
Making a shrine to yourself?

I expect most people would cringe at the thought of it,
But in actual reality no-one is more divine than you are.
For we are the whole of creation
and we created everything in existence.
I create my play – this life I live.
Every single experience I have is there by my command.
No-one is in charge out there or up above.

Awakening Humanity

If you stand in your true presence you are released
from the mental and emotional chains
Which imprison you and restrict the flow
of pure life force through you as a human being.

A billion stars are exploding inside us.
They are bursting forth, birthing new stars,
Solar systems, Galaxies, Universes.
We are the beginning and the ending.
We are all that ever has been and ever will be.
We can arise as radiant beings.
See and behold our magnificent natures.
No-one and nothing outside us.
There's just the one of us, always.
Boundaries, frontiers and limitations evaporate and dissolve
in this moment.
Gone.
Welcome into my world as I feel welcomed into yours.

Awakening Humanity

Our world.
I thank you,
Yes your selfless love which I experience in every moment of our life.
I acknowledge your perfection
And celebrate your wondrous beauty as a human, as a plant, as an animal, tree, river, star, cup of tea.

I kiss your feet in adoration.
Living God/esses all.
Right now,
just as we are.

For every pain I have ever suffered come now a thousand joys.
All the pleasure, ecstasy and love I have ever denied myself.
I let it envelop and permeate every atom of my being,
Your being and our being
Infinitely and eternally.

I appreciate your overwhelming beauty, wisdom, love,
all seeing-ness, truth,
and infinite eternal nature.

Awakening Humanity

Thank you for revealing this wonder to me –
for allowing me to see this sweet one that we all are.
I thank every single one of you who has ever lived,
is living and who will live in the future.

There are many levels of consciousness
which are waking up in all of us.

The blinkers are definitely slipping.

There is a massive increased interest in all things spiritual
and a whole new field of alternative therapies and energy healing.
We are recognizing that we are not just our bodies.
In fact we have many,
and some people can see or sense them naturally.
The children of today have a greater capacity
for seeing beyond the physical body than we did.

There is no taste like the taste of truth.
Everything other than this, pales into being an outer imitation
Trying to masquerade as the real thing.
Most people's lives today, are about either changing themselves,

their partners, or something in the world outside.
Perhaps if we can make it and be successful, famous, beautiful
or rich - then wouldn't that be great.
Everything will be sorted because now you've got what you need
to be happy and fulfilled.

Getting things, having experiences and having goals.
It's all outside and we want it.
Everything, and it never stops and its so relentless.
The media telling us what we need to be like and buy to be okay.
How are we going to get it all?
It's impossible.

We are the sum total of everything and everyone
that has been, is and will be.
At present most education, social institutions, politics and finance,
operate through the lens of personal mistaken identity.

No-one will ever achieve true security and completeness
by trying to manipulate others and outside circumstances.
As long as an individual sees themselves
as a separate subjective self

and experiences the world as separate from itself
there will be suffering and dissatisfaction.
All of our seeking, yearning, trying and dissatisfaction
is caused by the basic sense of incompleteness,
which is inevitable when experienced from a state of dualism.
We know that all external phenomena is transient.
Nothing stays the same from one moment to the next.
Our original and only true point of being
is our only reliable awareness.
That is constant and unchanging.
Self realization does not refer to an individual self or ego
to be realized or freed.

Your innate awareness is always the same
whatever is occurring in this world of convincing appearance.
When we wake up from sleep we know
that no matter how vivid
and seemingly real our dreams may have been
– we know it was just a dream and not what we consider real.
When we wake up to our true awareness we realize
that our entire life story and identity is actually a dream too.

Awakening Humanity

You are already that for which you are continuously seeking.
Any effort towards finding this pearl of consciousness
takes you immediately from what you are already in.
Any thought, feeling, mood, opinion
can accompany true consciousness.
It's not about stopping yourself from being just the way you are.
Not about changing anything.
This is non effort, relaxing and giving yourself a break.
This awareness has and does evade the human race.
We can wake up to the fact that as a species
we have been operating for millennia
using a fraction of our real intelligence.
No other animal on this planet destroys its own habitat.
Surely that is crazy.
We look to everything that's happening outside us
to see how we are doing.
Then we feel okay, not okay,
have to change, improve, or even give up.
A great big measuring stick always in the background.
It's set up for failure for everyone.
We don't know what's going on
and there are very few people around who can tell us.

Awakening Humanity

We are living as a miracle in a miracle, as a miracle.
Do most of us see this? No we see struggle, fear and limitation.
Our lives are enclosed by separation and division.
An imitation of closeness and intimacy
is often attempted by people
to give the impression of belonging to something.
Bigger than just them or their family or nationalistic identity.
We are born alone and die alone.
But at no instant of our lives could we possibly be alone.
ONLY our physical body appears separate.
We live in an ocean of appearances.
Bombarded by information.
Drowned into a trance.
Coping with this life.
Struggling to do everything and never meeting the targets.
Or maybe sometimes
Living a surface version of the true person you are.
The true human you are.
Pure awareness can only be experienced, not thought or felt.
Thought and feelings are temporary states
But reality is eternal.

Awakening Humanity

It's what is behind every single thing,
every appearance, thought, emotion, mood.
Authentic awareness is ever-present.
It's flooding everything constantly.
The world is already in perfect awareness of itself.

Sleeping Unawakened

Sleeping Unawakened

It's like a great a joke that we are all struggling
with the mistaken Hell of separateness.
We shift it around constantly but it never works.
It's because it's fake.
Sometimes it can appear very real – but it never works.

Everyday life being human.

You wake up, switch off the alarm clock off.

Don't want to go to work today or maybe
something good is expected so it might not feel that bad.
How automatic are you being?
Is everything coming from habit just like a programmed machine?
And are you living the present from memory
or fear or expectation of the future?
Or is it new and fresh and real,
each moment an unfolding of the unknown and a mystery?

And the person next to you in bed – your husband lover or wife.
Who are they?
How do you perceive them?

Sleeping Unawakened

Are your perceptions measured by recent events
and interactions with them?
Were you happy the last time you talked with them?
Where you in agreement
and did you experience feeling close and intimate with them?
or was there a distance between you?
Most of the time we are living in the past or the future
no matter what the situation, be it personal or work related.
If we were in the present and living from our true consciousness
our experience would be clean new and intimate.
It would reflect our true consciousness.
Many people have had momentary glimpses
of realness and true seeing,
Yet fail to live a life reflecting that.
They then remember it as a special occasion.
A magic and rare moment that came from outside them
and they usually attach it to some event that occurred
Often seeking to recreate it
by returning to the place where they experienced it,
or the teacher they were sitting with,
or the music they were listening to,
or the location that it happened at.

Sleeping Unawakened

The end of suffering and the beginning
of suffering are the same thing.

No one is a winner in a vale of tears.
Outcomes are never certain
and for most people goals are sought for,
died for and lived for.
Sometimes people live or die for the stories
and attachments of others.
They even commit crimes, or hurt others because of their belief
in the solidness and reality of something a leader said was true.
All of the stories end.
Everyone dies.
Everything changes at each moment.
The really important and key reason for us all
Is the thing that has become hidden – esoteric – mysterious –
veiled.
And it's the very thing which is actually the only valid reason
that life exists at all.

Sleeping Unawakened

Inside out and upside down world it is.
It's a stage in our human evolution,
a growing up emotionally and mentally.
Hampered by random emotions and thoughts
constantly telling us how to feel and what to think.
Constant drain of our energy.

Never being here,
never really listening to anyone –
and no-one ever hearing you.
Because they don't know who you are at all
Because they don't know themselves.
What is conversing with what, and who with who?
And for what agenda and hidden reasons?

The really great thing, though,
is that you are already okay,
totally fine in every way.
You cannot improve yourself in any way.

Trying to change yourself is a road to misery and disappointment.
You can never achieve real change

Sleeping Unawakened

If it's your mistaken identity you are working on.
All you do when you try to change,
is move, control, hide or suppress,
surface behaviour and patterns.

But the core stays the same –
so the outer can be altered
But the feelings deep inside reman the same.
Then life may get even worse.
When we listen to thoughts and feelings and outer feedback
to give us a reflection of how we are doing
we are relying on distorted feedback.
It's warped and inaccurate, just like a fairground mirror.
It's a reflection of our outer form but perceived in a distorted way.
There is no cliff nor sacrifice.
We are already home.
We just don't believe it.

Sleeping Unawakened

At an authentic level of true consciousness
all external phenomena are devoid of self or individual nature.
Self liberation in a real sense means that whatever manifests
in the arena of our awareness and is experienced
– is allowed to express just as it is.
No judgement, point of view or preference of liking or disliking.
If there is no attachment to whatever is manifesting around us,
no matter what it may be, and whatever we may think or feel about it,
it is then just free to be whatever is going on.
Practicing in this way the seeds and roots
of the erroneous tree of dualistic vision
never get a chance to sprout,
much less take root and grow.

So it's very practical and you can live an ordinary life
without rules and disciplines.
The only practice is to remain
in your own original authentic awareness
and integrate that state with whatever arises in you
and what is occurring around you moment to moment.
No-one need even know what you are practicing.
In fact this is the art of non-practice.

Sleeping Unawakened

This is the freedom we are seeking
But we usually go completely the wrong way about it.
Upside down and inside out way.
Our true and real natural condition is play.

Our innate consciousness
from which the whole of existence emerges,
the Earth, the animals and humans
in fact everything in existence is complete.
Because of a basic misconception we as consciousness as humans
have entered into the deluded state of duality or separation.

We mistakenly believe that everything we experience
is somehow outside of our true identity.
Because we think like this we are constantly trying to manipulate
the falsely perceived outside world.
Trying endlessly and, finally, unsuccessfully to bring to an end
the continual dissatisfaction and unease
which is the inevitable experience of obscured pure awareness.
This dissatisfaction continues even if we achieve worldly success
until we remember the awareness of our original state of grace.

Truth and Illusion

Truth and Illusion

It's the gap between the gaps of existence.
The gap which is no longer a gap.
The space where
separation is no longer an entertainable illusion.
Seeing, slicing through the distracting edges
of the fabrication
We, the jester, laughingly put up to convince ourselves
that we exist
As separate finite people –
With cleverly defined edges
Bagged up into individual bodies.

There are levels of perception that are being stroked
and interacted with Now
Which will blow the blinkered
View of life and reality –
As fostered by mass consciousness today.
Every day the machine keeps going, distracting,
tempting, luring, hypnotising,
tv, radio, internet...
Advertising denial of the truth.

Truth and Illusion

It's an upside down and inside out world we are living in.
Truth.
We are One.
We have lived for ever and will live forever more.

We perceive ourselves to come into a body
for a finite period of measured time,
Linear time.
As we integrate our consciousness into an individual form
That we have named
A human being Independent of each other.
This misconception has taken us into a forgetting of our oneness.
Everything in the Universe is interconnected,
We are just One Being.
The error is in believing we are just the Many.
To open yourself to nakedness and
Retain no defence at all is to embrace the real you
that's usually well hidden.
This isn't really scary.

We have come to believe that it is terrifying.
From the moment you were born,

Truth and Illusion

The outside world has fed you with a false reflection,
Stimulus and with feedback and expectations.
You are looking into a distorted mirror.
You are hardly ever receiving a true reflection.

We are all able to let go of all the lies
we have ignorantly taken on board
From the world we perceive as outside us.
The message seems to be like this –
You are never going to get it right no matter how hard you try.
Never going to be good enough,
slim enough, rich enough, strong enough,
enlightened enough, anything enough –
Your just not okay, the way you are.

So the false or mistaken identity essentially robs us
of our natural sense of total connection
As a whole and perfectly balanced true identity.
This mistaken identity is at the root of all dysfunction.
It is the perfect time right now to awaken
from this dream of separation.

Truth and Illusion

A dream where everyone and everyone's lives have seemingly and
mistakenly separate existences.
The individual 'I', is non-existent – yet it exists
It is an illusion which is accepted by the majority of humanity.
What we think and feel is what we identify with
and colours the quality of our lives.
We try to seek out and cultivate nice and pleasant experiences
And avoid the unpleasant and unwanted ones.
For brief times you may have experienced
success, admiration, your heart's desire.
Yet it never lasts for ever.

Many people become frightened that they will then lose
what they have strived so hard to achieve,
and have become so attached to their enhanced identity –
That they will act in a harmful way to themselves,
or others to protect it.

At the end of the day we all die
– our existence in a body is finite
But in truth, as the eternal consciousness that we are,
we live forever.

Truth and Illusion

Just as the individual lives of planets and solar systems is finite.
Anything in any type of form is finite.
Humanity has barely touched on or experienced
the potential within itself –
Even on the finite levels,
of which there are many layers of manifestation.

The physical level of form is the slowest moving
and the last place, in the many bodies we move about in,
Where complete alignment with the core truth level occurs.
This is not dependent on anything from the outside,
The outside circumstances do not matter at all
As true awareness can spontaneously arise
within anyone anywhere, anytime.
In a crowd
– on your own – in any life situation.

Nothing outside of you can help you to experience the real.
The real you does not belong to anything or anyone.
It's going to be okay and it doesn't matter at all
what your past life has been about.
Reality is not interested in it.

Truth and Illusion

In fact, it's got nothing to do with it.
The kindest person on the planet and the cruelest
are no different to each other at the core.
They are the same.

Being real is not about anything you have thought was you.
Yet the real beauty waiting to love you totally
In a way you've never been loved before,
Is the only thing that s worth being with and sharing.
The rest of you is conditional and it always has an agenda,
or a position, opinion or an identity to maintain,
That's the bottom line.
We start to believe we are the caricature personalities
we have created and trapped ourselves in
And lived our lives as.

When real love occurs its got nothing to do with the you
that you normally are and identify with.
Real love cannot be controlled
And we lose our sense of self in our familiar way –
And let go of control –
and surrender to something unknown and new.

Truth and Illusion

Love, real love, is always new.
Most of what we experience everyday is an old experience.
Our brains are nothing less than information sensors recording
everything through our senses.
Each memory is compared to a previous memory
and so on and so on.
Gradually we become less and less able to be new and fresh
And incapable of experiencing life as new and real and as it is.
Now.
Mostly it's got nothing to do with the present –
Because we are not here.
We are in a version of the past or some fantasy or terror
of the as yet unlived future.
So in truth, who we are accustomed to thinking and feeling we are
is redundant.

Home
Falling back into the consciousness of original grace –
It's what we already are.
We are all nothing short of total perfection.
Through our limited senses, we humans struggle to make sense
of our lives on Earth –

Truth and Illusion

This perceived time as a somebody.
For a lot of people it's not an enjoyable experience.
Experiences of pain often results in someone closing down
from the outside world –
Thus inhibiting and limiting present connection with realness,
And true and authentic awareness of reality.
True relating to people, animals and nature becomes infrequent.
Fear taints everything.
The individual can live only through the lens of the past
and fear of the future –
Or glamourising the past and fearing the future
will never be as good again.
Everyone going around living a non-present existence.
Most of us living through a filter of past events
and distorted memories.

Realness is rare but when experienced even for a moment
one's perspective is pierced.
It slices through the layers of unrealness and distorted memory
like a knife through butter.

Truth and Illusion

Most of us try to improve, grow, change or seek to present
an enhanced identity to ourselves and to other people.
Trying to make ourselves better.
So many fix it up strategies these days.
Take your pick.

This can be on any level from the physical right through
to the emotional, mental or etheric energy bodies.
Spiritual improvement too.

Being better than others is also socially encouraged on every level.
Being best at something.
An idea which is born from separation.
This is all to feed the false identity and
distorted sense of individuality.
So much distortion is going on in the world around us too.
If the initial false identity of our everyday consciousness
is what we look to for instructions
— then nothing will feel right for very long.

As a whole we are not accessing and living from
our pure and true consciousness.

Truth and Illusion

Very few people in the world are willing or able to do this
– up until now,
And the ironic thing is that it is the most simple thing in the world.
Innate intelligence reveals truth.
Is truth.
The whole thing has become mysterious and rare.
Yet this consciousness has been witnessed and written about
for many thousands of years
all over the world.

It's right in front, at each side
and below and above us.

It's what we already are.
Nothing to look for or sort out or improve.
Eternity and infinity is ever-present everywhere.

We are what we most seek.
In fact the only thing we ever really want.
Everything else eventually loses any real satisfaction,
True satisfaction.
True Freedom.

Truth and Illusion

Now that's what we all want.
Freedom and truth.
Today the few that have somehow simply 'gone home'
Often become seen as objects of reverence
and mistakenly made into special people.
This is exactly what a person who is aware is not.
He or she is simply being their true self
with nothing added or taken away.
They have achieved nothing at all.
They have given up looking and stopped believing
that they are not already fine.

The lie began, when you identified yourself
as a separate, unconnected consciousness only.
It's one of the most untrue things you can ever think or believe.
It's ridiculously awful for anyone to deal with,
because it is so far removed from truth.
Removed from flow and alignment, with yourself.
So far removed from you, as you really are.
It's a lot to deal with, this being a human business.

Truth and Illusion

The lie – it's just me –
Oh no! what happened?
How did I get here?
What is this body?
And where did it come from?

Why am I 'me' and not someone else?
Doesn't make any sense at all does it?
Even writing this now, there is sometimes a feeling of thinking
Is this okay?
And have I got this right?
Like I have to score a certain amount of brownie points.
And there is an authority watching over me
judging and assessing me –
Like there is a perfect thing to be or to reach.
Something outside of me – the observer.
It's all an illusion.
You just have to be okay with You and that's it.
You have to just sort it with You.
No one can judge you,
They are only able to be okay with themselves.

Truth and Illusion

This is the opposite of the outer world.
So much pressure to be alright – but by what standards?
And from where and for what?
But be aware that all this is irrelevant
and is not worth pursuing, for one moment.

Allow the fears and the nightmares,
And at the same time know that you are the beauty
you have always sought
At every moment of your lives.

The outer play and experience are but a mirage and distraction,
From being at home with yourself.
Simply being fine, completely content
And complete – in just being.
Dropping and dropping deeper, and deeper,
into the warm embracing softness of yourself.
This is only the beginning of meeting
Your true beloved and being met by them.
For in reality we have no name, no shape,
no colour, no religion, no sex,
No distinction from anything else.

Truth and Illusion

It's just an invented story that is definitely not you –
Who you are.
You are none of that.

When you stop identifying with that invented person
Then you can actually have the possibility of going home.
Living a life that's real, healthy and natural.
It is the real and natural you who will welcome you home.
So many people in the West are suffering
from stress and depression.
Often medication just suppresses the symptoms
of mistaken identity syndrome.

Everyone has times when life seems too hard to bear.
It's often at these times that we wonder what it's all about.
It's not about everything going wrong.
Are we here just to have a bad time,
with hope of some happiness occasionally,
to keep us going?
Is there a really cruel God up there
having a damn good laugh at making us suffer?
No, I know that is not true.

Truth and Illusion

Real intimacy – true intimacy – is the true relationship
between all that lives.
It's honoring the true connection between all life.
We are one life, split into billions of temporary bodies and forms.
The truth is that there is one consciousness alone;
It's not separate,
and we only appear to have separate consciousnesses.
If all of our awareness was awakened and fully functioning,
then we would be able to witness that we are one intelligence.
Our core true intelligence is fully aware
of the complete state of union between all life.

This is not cosmic religious pie in the sky escapism
but scientific fact.

The external world is constantly changing.
Everything just seems to happen to you,
no matter how much you try to control your existence.
The more you wake up, the more you become aware
that life is like a dream.
When you awake you see that the you up to this point has been
at the mercy of your own personal dream

Truth and Illusion

– lived as though real
– by you the sleeper.

You the authentic seer with totally clear vision
sees that this dream can be discarded
And that instead you can now start to live increasingly
in your true consciousness.
True consciousness sees all form as a temporary drama.
You the authentic seer will lose nothing that's real.
You will have access instead to your true consciousness.
That in turn sets you free to live the life you were born to live.

To express yourself fearlessly, and to shine
And be celebrated back by the entire Universe.
That's not the case, right now in this world.
How can anyone truly celebrate anyone or anything,
without it being tainted by some strategy?

The thing is that people recognise truth outside of themselves
Sometimes more easily, when they see it
In the form of a beautiful sunset, or an innocent babe,
or an awake person.

Truth and Illusion

Often people then mistake the person or object
as the goal or answer.
Their personal view of themselves is so distorted
and seen through the eyes of past experience,
That they cannot entertain the thought
that they are also that perfect too
And in reality everything is perfect.
Its our messing with everything that takes us way
from what already is perfection.
You showed them a glimpse of home.
The baby you was untainted by distortion and fear.
Conditioning and history had barely touched you.

Always knew that I was as simple as a blade of grass or drop of rain.
I knew that no-one was more special than anyone else.
In the end we all died,
and we all come into incarnation through the sex act.
Yes we all get colds, worry, have complexes, and feel insecure.
We are just human after all.

Do we have to be special or do superhuman feats
to deserve to be here?

Truth and Illusion

It's a tough call all round to meet every demand
that this world seems to require of us.

Merging into everything.
Or that's what I describe it as but actually, we are everything.
In reality there is no merging as I am already
what I experience merging into.
Just been suffering the illusion of separation.
Worse than any sickness of the body.
Discovering that my edges are nowhere near
where I thought they were.
Thought my edges were where my body ended
but now I find that they are the cloth of the Universe
and are infinite threads of the Divine fabric of life itself.

What a thrill, a beautiful ecstatic thrill of knowing
that all the doom and gloom and fear is not real.
Knowing and being with the inner stillness and calm
that fills all existence
If you are just open to hear it, feel it, embrace it and know it as You.
Your existence knows no edges.
It has no beginning or endings.

Cosmic Consciousness

Heart Awareness

Cosmic Awareness - Heart Awareness

It's like getting off the cycle.
Everything stops and is replaced
by a previously unimagined beauty and vastness.
Every face is your own as you spread out and envelop
and merge with everything.
Everyone is in a loving relationship with you.
You are in love with life.
All boundaries disappear and the Universe is contained within you,
Within everyone and everything.
Your experience is of love pulsating
and vibrating powerfully in every cell
of your being.
Inclusiveness is your only true awareness.
Total openness.
You see yourself everywhere.
Awe.
Wonder, humility and love.
No observer, no wants or needs or exclusion.

Your heart feels like a stream of love flowing out
and receiving at the same time.

Cosmic Awareness - Heart Awareness

This is totally letting go and surrendering to what you really are
as a human being.
Closeness and recognition of the communion of every living thing.
The sacredness of yourself.
The wholeness of yourself and the perfection
of your every moment of existence.
And everything is living.
Everything in existence is yourself.

Joy, bliss and the sweetest ecstasy imaginable.
Relax and rest in yourself on every level,
whatever may be happening
As it will all pass, whether it be joy, hate, fear or happiness.
Whatever your thoughts and feelings may be at any given moment
They are temporary and influenced
by either outer goings-on at the time
Or memories, or some future imagined scenario.

In this resting state, which is without effort,
Linear time is replaced by eternity.
No effort, no attachment, no dialogue or analysis.
Stillness and a deep, quiet intimacy with who you truly are.

Cosmic Awareness - Heart Awareness

Thus intimacy with all life –
For that's what you are.
Already are, and always have been.

You remember and know now that there are no divisions
and that separation is an illusion.

Loneliness is untrue and is borne from misconception
and mistaken identity.
It's a tragic error.
Loneliness comes from the false belief
that we are alone in some way.
Our identity and sense of 'I'-ness
Are tied up in our sense of 'me'.
All discomfort and suffering are rooted in this false attachment
to a separate self.
This mistaken belief in a personal identity is at the core of all pain.
Separation begins here and warps the whole of human lives.
Many spiritual and religious teachers have emphasized
the unity of all life.
Of all existence.
Accepting yourself totally.

Cosmic Awareness – Heart Awareness

Whatever is going on around you,
Remain in the simple is-ness of life.
Moment to moment.
You are not only what is occurring, what you are thinking, feeling,
planning or remembering,
But your true consciousness.

What would be of benefit to all of us
– the One that we are –
To know Ourselves.
Is there a key or a bridge which connects the human with the being?

It is the heart.
That's where both connect, where both find union.
Here in our own inner bosom we can find peace and rest.

The human heart has the capacity for enormous love
which takes nothing for the temporary falsely claimed self.
By embracing our true natures,
we discover that we are everyone and all that exists,
has existed
and all that will come into form.

Cosmic Awareness - Heart Awareness

We are eternal and infinite beings.
We are all inclusive.

Spiritual and physical are the same.
They are not separate.
The soul and the body are one.

The real us never dies or gets so lost that it is destroyed.
This is no narcissistic theory.
Narcissism is a distortion of true identity
which is mistaken by an individual person.
Even great awareness can be stolen by the ego

and claimed for itself as its own possession.
True consciousness realizes that it owns nothing.
It has no need of anything outside of itself,
because it is the sum total of existence.
True seeing knows love in a complete way.
As the human heart opens and surrenders to awareness
It opens to the seeing that this heart is the size of the Universe
And is contained within all life.

Cosmic Awareness - Heart Awareness

Our hearts are the truth and our hearts know what we are.
We see that our temporary forms and our life stories
are just the tip of the iceberg.
No amount of mental understanding will ever reveal
the absolute truth to us.

I feel my heart including all life and I soar with the bird in flight,
Gurgle with the stream,
Feel cold like the earth,
And emerge from the ground like a spring flower.
We are all this.
We are all of us, fully conscious human beings.

What beauty and wonder is our great inheritance
that we have laid in store for ourselves one day.
The pot of true gold does exist,
and it belongs to everyone.

At some point we are all Winners
and it's better than X factor or the lottery.
To be in our human form

Cosmic Awareness - Heart Awareness

Yet have his consciousness of being life itself.
What a blessed thing.
People who have realized something of their true nature
are changed people.
They continue in an individual body
yet their awareness begins to include more of the truth in their lives.
They start to live in a new way,
and they are increasingly aware of being a universal consciousness.
A truly inspiring and very human being.
We do not have to be saints or be perfect.
We don't have to do a particular type of job or never swear.

We don't have to change anything.
We are already standing at our destination.
In this world
That is possible.

We are human and somehow we gain in practice
At merging our true consciousness with our human lives.

Cosmic Awareness - Heart Awareness

And this is accomplished through an open heart
Dropping your awareness into your heart
and surrendering to its knowing.

We are all very different and unique expressions
of the one that we all are.
Each one of us is as valuable and divine as anyone else.
What a fabulous exchange - bargain of eternity.

Never been an offer like it or will there be.

The offer is free and available now.

You give up fear, dread, loneliness,
self deception and manipulation,

And instead live from a place of love,
perceiving one-ness and union
Everywhere and with everyone.
Whenever you are not relaxing you are holding fear.
That's why healing sometimes feels painful.
Letting go and giving up is a huge and beautiful key.

Cosmic Awareness - Heart Awareness

Accessing the one that you are is more available.
And who doesn't want that?

Baby, baby. let that huge sun inside you shine out
and be felt by all creation
And let them know and share It with you,
Giving and receiving in effortless flow.

Opening up – resting in your heart, and simply relaxing into the
experience you are in –
Is a wise move.
Be still in your personal experience and be present.

Be like Neo in The Matrix – still in the middle of attackers –
and have choice about how you experience each moment.
Awake and present and at ease.

You can experience one-ness and flow or separation and fear,
history, reaction and patterns.

The awakening You will become free and fearless,
Entering a fresh and true way of living.

Cosmic Awareness - Heart Awareness

Living authentically,
independently of your mind, emotions,
personal identity, sexuality and life history.
Having the ability to live fully in the moment
- whatever the life situation.
Ever present, ever constant
and one hundred percent loyal to you,
always.

It is the Pretender who steals your true consciousness.
The trickster with its many moods and faces
and opinions and dramas.
The world mistakenly
Believes the Pretender to be the real them –
Think that their real awareness is special,
weird, glamorous, spiritual, mystical, etc.

Many people feel that awareness
has to be achieved and efforted for.
That something special 'happens to them' rarely
And must be sought after,

Cosmic Awareness - Heart Awareness

Discovered and be found, and held onto.
And in this quest
The pot of gold becomes elusive –
and somehow unattainable.
That's because the Pretender tries to steal it back –
When actually it's already ours
And it's what we are already
And no trying is necessary.

The Pretender we think is us –
Our pieced together identity
Based on what we have deduced to have happened
to us in the past
And formulated into a picture of a self –
We are not that.
We are the awareness we seek,
the perfection, love and authenticity of pure life force itself.
And that is why we are here.
To know and be with ourselves authentically.
Paradise is the core of you.
Everything else is a distortion of perfection.

Being Home

Being Home

We as a species are actually already home now,
Relaxing in our 'inner home' –
The only home which belongs equally to all of us,
which we all share –
is a wonderful state of human experience.
It's the crowning glory of our existence.

Once a person becomes anchored within this place,
All the rest of the person starts to become transformed
And the quality of their authentic nature shines through them.
There is nothing like it,
and it is impossible to compare it to anything else.
Here all comparisons are gone.
There is the awareness of One –
a boundary-less inner resting place.
You and your source merge.
Yet they have always been unseparated.

You really know that you are settled
in a way you have always hungered for
It has previously never been completely met, outside of you before.
True identity is brilliant.

Being Home

Keep returning to it, and allow it to embrace you
and wrap you in its loving, tender arms.
We are all already home.
Everything is home.
It's the only thing that's real.

We are just under a great misunderstanding.
It's as if humanity is having a massive resistance to true seeing.

This sweet nectar wants nothing and it has nothing to give.
It's the purest, clearest and truest thing you can ever experience.
It's you.
It's not an experience –
It's what you are.

If someone is at home they have no interest in owning or possessing
anything or anyone –
As at home you know that you are already everything in existence.

There are no paths here and no trips either.
Your identity as you have known yourself to be, can be embraced,
Allowing your true awareness to be witness to life,

Being Home

as it really and truly is.
We are bombarded with innumerable distractions which call us
at every moment – all demanding our undivided attention.
There is a core of us which knows them to be distortions of reality.
This inner centre never changes,
It's just there waiting for you.

A peace you have sensed and always sought.
Always longing for your visit which can be for a moment
or forever.
You are in love with
Expressing your real nature
And relaxing effortlessly into what is occurring around you.
Cherishing and belonging, and being your true innermost self.
We are all unconsciously being called back home at each moment
We often think that our glimpses into reality come from outside,
And we seek to reconstruct the outer situation,
in which we tasted that,
which we always have longed for.
It never works though.
Because it happened all by itself, effortlessly.

Being Home

You can never reach the real by manipulating the outside world,
people or conditions.
The real is what you are already.
You are totally okay and fine right now.

Home is where true and complete relaxation is found.
Every moment you go home,
everything in existence connects with your knowing.
I absolutely know one hundred percent who you are.
Sometimes it feels so overwhelmingly beautiful.
Stay calm and still and at rest in your heart.

Stop grabbing and seeking and searching.
What you hunger for is within you. It's here right now.

Relax and be and remember your baby smile.
This is the Holy Grail, Heaven, Nirvana, Samadhi,
Ecstasies, bliss and all the names which describe truth.
It's not grand and it's not out of this world.
It's about being in this world as you are and as it is really.
We have been searching all our lives
for this fantastic and sacred state.

Being Home

There in reality is nothing anyone actually seeks.
All other seeking is in imitation of the true prize.
It costs nothing that is of value.
It costs everything that is not authentic.
This is a peace and silence which cuts through everything
that you believed yourself to be.
Peace of mind, peace of emotions,
peace in the heart and peace in the body.
Everything is just fine.
Contentedness.
Contentless.
Becoming aware of your innermost self is so beautiful.
It wants nothing at all.
It does not crave.
It is still.
It has no beliefs, prejudices, preferences.
It possesses nothing.
There is no other.
There are no others.
Oneness is.
You are One-ness.

Being Home

You no longer see only through the eyes of an individual,
But through the eyes of the Beloved lover who is in love,
In conscious union with all.

Your ears hear the divine synthesis of universal harmony.
Sound can be felt through the skin, the organs, the body.

Home

Stillness within
Expression of flow

The mind cannot comprehend stillness.
The mind can be still yet not comprehend it.
The mind comprehends movement.
We know yet cannot understand.
To be in absolute stillness yet still do.

At home – living in what you know is real.
Vibrant with real life.
Your awareness knowing what actually is.

Being Home

The illusion is that you have to keep doing things
and getting more and more stuff,
no matter what type of stuff it is, because when you stop
it's empty inside.
Usually you manifest something and create your own reality.
You also have to protect it.
Then everybody's self reality will compete with yours.
Separation.

Love and Intimacy

Love and Intimacy

When two people are open to the core
of real consciousness within themselves
And they remain open and energetically connected with each other,
A new and true love can be experienced.
This is when truth meets real love.
Whole consciousness.
Awakened consciousness meets authentic relationship.
Here in this fragile tender space,
true intimacy and real communication can occur –
And the awesomeness of this confirms for the experiencer
That they and the other person
Are one and the same.
It's often referred to as merging.
In actual fact there is no merging,
as we are already everyone and everything.

It's a shift away from the separate 'I'.
In merging we have an intimate alignment
of all our bodies with another,
And the realization that we are the same being as someone else.

Love and Intimacy

This experience is very real and strengthens our connection
with our core intelligence.
Truth is very simple.
It's all of us in our present human evolution of self awareness.
Many people are awakened or have had experiences
of realness in varying degrees.
Some people then attach these experiences
to mystical or religious meaning.
This only puts clutter back
on top of truth and real natural awareness.
It's only when you stand naked in emptiness,
That means without your personal identity, your history,
your possessions, your relationships, job, body image –
Every thing that gives you a sense of you.

There is so much space here.
So much room and presence in the moment.
Just experience your true consciousness witnessing itself.
Falling – in – loveness.

The pure ecstasy of just merging with another, be it a person,
animal, plant, mountain, lake or star.

Love and Intimacy

Completion of your true self can be found everywhere.
Yet you are already complete now.
Openness is just fantastically right.
When immersed in your real awareness,
the revelation that anything but this seeing
Is a distorted version of reality.
Two people who are not at home
in themselves experience in the other,
the same lack of consciousness in each other.
Two sets of patterns, needs, wants
and desires interact with each other.
What is real in our relationships? What is being met?
If it's just the outer false identities relating,
true intimacy will not occur.
These relationships can merely be a mirror for the lack in you.
When two people who are at home
in themselves connect with each other
an authentic relationship is possible.
At present very few people have neither the opportunity
nor the courage to face that sort of realness in their lives.
Free-falling, free-falling and not stopping.
Nothing here ever changes.

Love and Intimacy

A connection which is true and unconditional
because it just is.
It's true and clean and wide open.
Poets try to convey this mysterious sense of connection
with everything.
Underneath our daily and nightly dream state
is the true reality of Oneness and unity.
Mystics have described this state as many wondrous things.
Nectar, peace, wholeness of experience.

In this state of natural perfection as a human being
a different relationship with all life can be experienced
right through all of our bodies
– not just the physical one
The senses become enraptured
by the new intimacy of relationship
with not just yourself
but with all around you.
When a bird flies across the sky you are flying as the bird
– you are one with it –
And when the wind blows

Love and Intimacy

you move within it
And you dance together as you are re-united
with your original consciousness.
The ability to merge with people, nature,
in fact anything in existence, is automatic.
The mind becomes freed to know truth
and no longer finds division,
strategies to defend the fictional 'I'.

When you look into the eyes of another
you see that you are one and the same consciousness.

You are no longer looking at a person and analyzing them
and assessing what you might get from them
or locking into some behavioural pattern with them.

Now you really see them for who they truly are
and can consciously experience your Oneness
as the only real true love there is.
It's like merging each into the other completely
and bathing in true awareness.

www.ingramcontent.com/pod-product-compliance
Lightning Source LLC
Chambersburg PA
CBHW050438010526
44118CB00013B/1577